# Nonsense
# Fairytale
# Rhymes

D1493013

*To Mo and Ella  K. U.*
*To Vineeta and Anisha, with love  C. F.*

**OXFORD**
UNIVERSITY PRESS

Great Clarendon Street, Oxford OX2 6DP

Oxford University Press is a department of the University of Oxford.
It furthers the University's objective of excellence in research, scholarship,
and education by publishing worldwide in

Oxford  New York
Auckland  Cape Town  Dar es Salaam  Hong Kong  Karachi
Kuala Lumpur  Madrid  Melbourne  Mexico City  Nairobi
New Delhi  Shanghai  Taipei  Toronto

With offices in

Argentina  Austria  Brazil  Chile  Czech Republic  France  Greece
Guatemala  Hungary  Italy  Japan  Poland  Portugal  Singapore
South Korea  Switzerland  Thailand  Turkey  Ukraine  Vietnam

Oxford is a registered trade mark of Oxford University Press
in the UK and in certain other countries

Text copyright © Kaye Umansky 2006
Illustrations copyright © Chris Fisher 2006

The moral rights of the author and artist have been asserted

Database right Oxford University Press (maker)

First published in 2006

British Library Cataloguing in Publication Data available

ISBN-13: 978-0-19-911233-3
ISBN-10: 0-19-911233-9

1 3 5 7 9 10 8 6 4 2

Printed in Thailand by Imago

# Nonsense Fairytale Rhymes

Poems by *Kaye Umansky*
*Illustrated by* Chris Fisher

OXFORD
UNIVERSITY PRESS

# Aladdin
# Made Short

The cave was dark,
The cave was damp.
Aladdin rubbed
The rusty lamp.

Alas, the genie
Never came.
Wrong lamp.
What a shame.

(He's down there still,
I must report.
And so this poem's
Very short.)

## Pea Poem

They piled up twenty mattresses,
But still she felt the pea.
She woke up in the morning
Feeling sore as sore can be.
She was just a mass of bruises,
They were purple, blue, and red.
It's really not a good idea
To have a pea in bed.

# Slimy Hearts

WANTED – a princess to give me a kiss.
I'm sick to the flippers of looking like this.

I'm slimy and green and I live down a well
Since a rotten old witch put me under a spell.

I'm really a prince, though I look like a frog.
You'll see what I mean when we get to the snog.

Please send me a photo of you in your crown
And we'll meet for The Kiss by the fountain in town.

Let's make it tomorrow at twenty past three.
(I'll be wearing a rose so you'll know that it's me.)

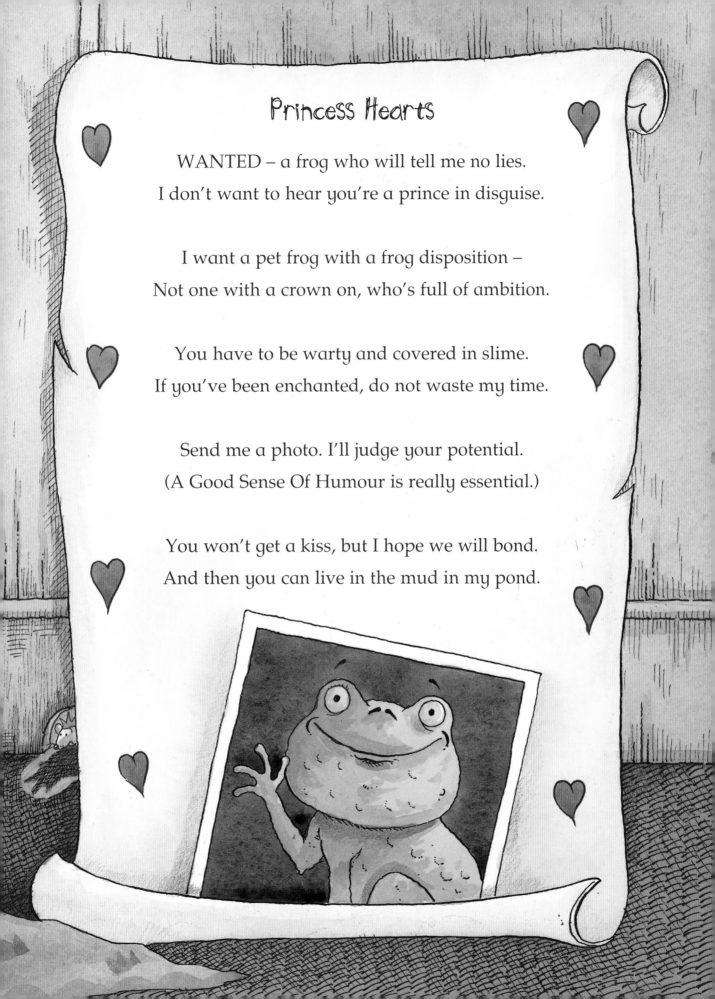

# Princess Hearts

WANTED – a frog who will tell me no lies.
I don't want to hear you're a prince in disguise.

I want a pet frog with a frog disposition –
Not one with a crown on, who's full of ambition.

You have to be warty and covered in slime.
If you've been enchanted, do not waste my time.

Send me a photo. I'll judge your potential.
(A Good Sense Of Humour is really essential.)

You won't get a kiss, but I hope we will bond.
And then you can live in the mud in my pond.

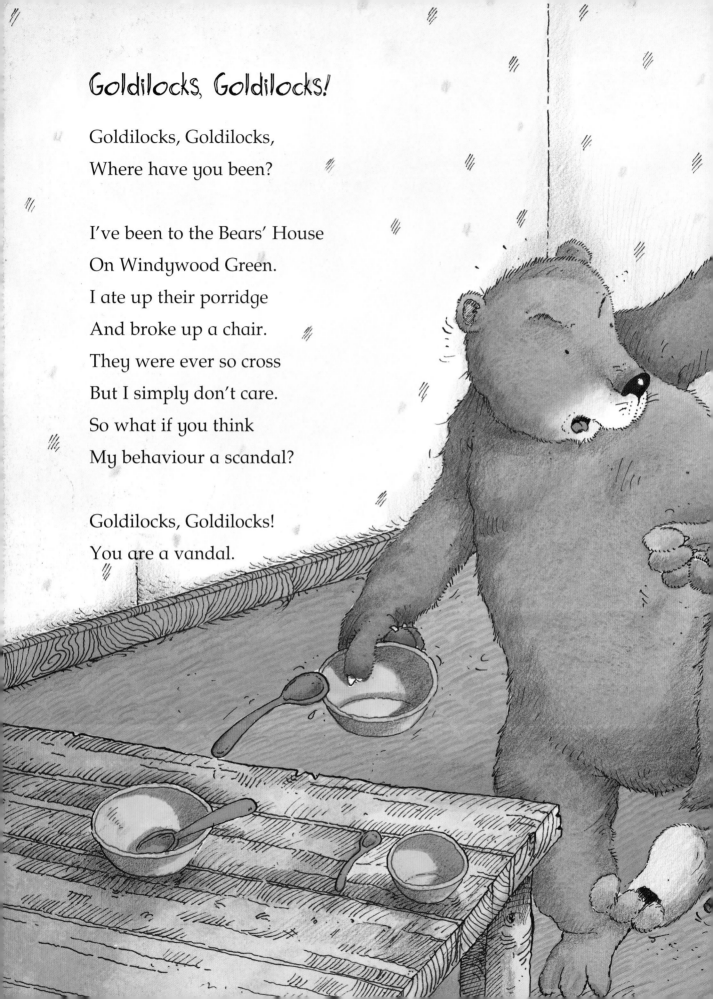

# Goldilocks, Goldilocks!

Goldilocks, Goldilocks,
Where have you been?

I've been to the Bears' House
On Windywood Green.
I ate up their porridge
And broke up a chair.
They were ever so cross
But I simply don't care.
So what if you think
My behaviour a scandal?

Goldilocks, Goldilocks!
You are a vandal.

# Cinderella Made Short

Cinderella at the ball,

Dancing with the prince.

The prince kept stepping on her toes.

He hasn't seen her since.

# Bad Luck Duck

This ugly duckling had no luck.

He grew into an ugly duck.

## Song of the Sweet House Witch

I'm building a house of sweets, tra la!
I'm building a house of sweets!
I'm going to put up a sign, tra la!
*THIS WAY – EATS!*

I'll hide inside in the dark, tra la!
I'll giggle and suck my thumb,
And licketty lick on a cinnamon stick
While I wait for the kiddies to come.

A nice little girl with curls, tra la,
Singing her merry wee song,
Or her fatter big brother who can't find his mother,
Whichever one comes along.

Ooooooh . . .

The kiddies'll come from miles around
To give my house a suck.
And that's my evil plan, tra la!
Wish me lots of luck!

## The Giant's Widow

I am the Giant's widow.
My husband won't be back.
He toppled off the beanstalk
When chasing after Jack.
I told him not to bother.
I told him, 'Stay in bed.
That boy will be the death of you,
I know he will,' I said.
Of course he didn't listen,
He knew his time had come.
I sometimes miss his fee a bit,
But not his fi, fo, fum.

# The Dwarfs of Snow White Fame

We are the dwarfs of Snow White fame
We're tellin' the truth to you,
We've twiddled our thumbs since the weddin',
We ain't got nuthin' to do.

Since the happy endin',
Everything's gone flat,
We can't go back to the gold mines,
We're much too grand for that.

The papers say we've had our day,
We beg to disagree.
We're very cute and cuddly
As anyone can see.

And so we're formin' a boy band,
We thought you'd like to know.
We hope you buy the record.
Hi ho, hi ho, hi ho!

## The Wolf's Song

I do a huff puff here!
A huff puff there!
Huff, puff, huff, puff,
Little pig, beware!
I'm big and bad and wolfy
And I want a bite to eat,
Bet you'll go down a treat!
Oooh! Huffy puffy puffy!
Ooooh! Huffy puffy puffy!
Ooooh! Watch me do my stuff-y!
Nice little pig, just
Ripe to eat!

# Troll Song

I'm a troll! (Troll, troll!)

I lives beneath! (Splash, splash!)

I rolls me eyes! (Roll, roll)

I gnash me teeth! (Gnash, gnash!)

I flex me claws! (Flex, flex!)

I sings me song! (La la!)

And I jumps out with a ROAR

When a billy goat comes along!

## RRRAAARRR!

# Rapunzel Complains

My name, it is Rapunzel
And there's nothing makes me madder
Than folks who use my hairdo
In the absence of a ladder.

I tell them not to do it
But they just don't seem to care.
I wonder how they'd like it
If I abseiled down *their* hair?

# Rumpelstiltskin Complains

They could have called me Gary,
Or Tom, or Tim, or Ted,
Or Will or Phil or Big Cool Bill,
Or John, or Jim, or Fred.
They could have plumped for Harry,
Or Rob, or Bob, or Brad –
But they named me Rumpelstiltskin,
Thanks for nothing, Mum and Dad.

You really cannot blame me
If I acted really mean
When I tried to take the baby
From that rather silly queen.
They called me Rumpelstiltskin,
And I'm cross about it still.
Just blame my dopey parents
Who should have called me Bill.

# What Makes the News

A Puss in Boots won't make the news
But what about A Dog in Shoes?

An Elephant Who Sings the Blues?
A Camel Who Can Mend a Fuse?

A Posh Gorilla on a Cruise?
A Stoat Who Likes to Wait in Queues?

Happy Flying Kangaroos?
Ballet-dancing Cockatoos?

Ducks Who Hold Good Barbecues?
Cows Who Won't Give Interviews?

What will make the news?
You choose.

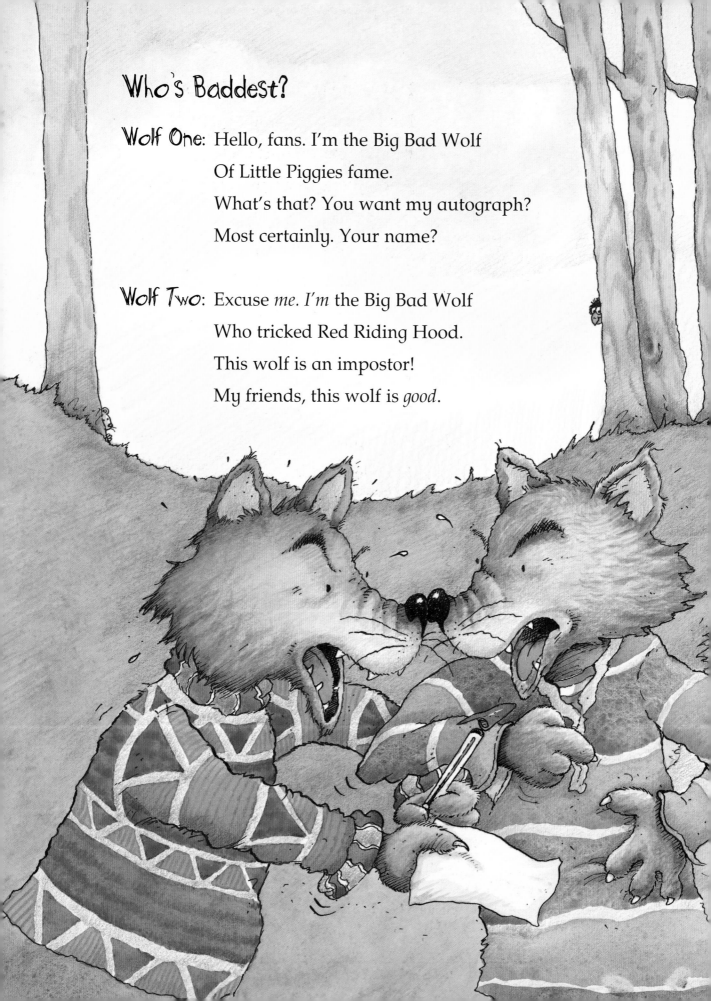

# Who's Baddest?

**Wolf One:** Hello, fans. I'm the Big Bad Wolf

Of Little Piggies fame.

What's that? You want my autograph?

Most certainly. Your name?

**Wolf Two:** Excuse *me. I'm* the Big Bad Wolf

Who tricked Red Riding Hood.

This wolf is an impostor!

My friends, this wolf is *good.*

**Wolf One:** How dare you. *I'm* the Big Bad Wolf
No matter what you say.
Be off, before I huff and puff
And blow you clean away.

**Wolf Two:** Aha! And so it's come to blows!
This wolf is really sad.
I'll go and eat his granny up
And *then* we'll see who's bad.
Huff, puff . . .
Gobble, gobble . . .
Huff, puff . . .
Gobble, gobble . . .
Huff, puff . . .
Gobble, gobble . . .

**Wolf One and Wolf Two:**
*Then* we'll see who's bad!

# The Gingerbread Boy

Said the Gingerbread Boy
To the Marshmallow Girl,
'Shall we go to a dance?
Do you fancy a twirl?'

Said the Marshmallow Girl
To the Gingerbread Boy,
'What, dance with a biscuit?
I don't think I'll risk it.'

### Hare's Farewell

How could I let him beat me?
Why did I go to sleep?
How could I act so boastful?
Why was I such a creep?
I'm leaving on the midnight train,
I cannot stay in town.
I let a tortoise beat me
And I'll never live it down.